forward

-nandini tiwari

to do more, to be more

Dear reader,

Life unfolds in fleeting moments

But today, let us linger here, *in the present*
these poems reflect love, nature, growth, and the simple joys life
brings,
reminding you that *life is not a destination but a dance....*

...celebrating the beauty of impermanence and the magic of
presence

welcome to "forward"

live fully and love deeply, here, and now.

nandini tiwari

from end to end
my eyes, with pride
embrace a world where love, steeped in memory
promises warmth within me

forward

nandini tiwari

with the scars i've carried all my life
distance becomes my healer
while the mirror remains a deceiver

forward

nandini tiwari

some people hold but a single line
and you're not the one to make it rhyme

forward

if love can fade, then all things must
even the strongest bonds return to dust

the years pass by
so learn to trust

for in each heart
you're still the first

4

forward

i rage, i burn, my heart's on fire
you draw me near, i quell desire

forward

just my little finger
wrapped in quiet ways
it's joy
a happiness that no one can ever destroy

forward

nandini tiwari

you'd know love's endless art
where we never part

forward

i've got a little habit of your smile
a silent promise
that our souls will always meet

forward

we danced in days
and built
a song

lucky in love
but always wrong

forward

to write my own story
i weave the dreams of others
lost without my soul
i chase hopes and fears

forward

and no one will look at us
living in empty fields, alone
or in another life
with a damaged mind

the world won't pause
the chaos will spin, relentless and wild
until you find a love for self
and call it home
(be its home)

forward

how can i fight with my fate
when it's written in the stars
and time just won't wait?

forward

searching for love in a world that feels so wide
i ask our souls to not collide

forward

if you dream
with a child's innocence
and wield words
like magic
you are both
healer and destroyer

forward

one thing was beautiful, the other a slip
the story has ended, yet i miss you still

forward

nandini tiwari

for years it has been chaos and not home

forward

want us to dance together
to love's playful rhythms and the jarring beats of
our passions
as life moves forward through the melody of our
existence

forward

forward

in borrowed tales of others
two hearts entwined
it's different but its love so true
and that's how destined paths collide

never before had i left summer behind
waiting for a monday
leaving flowers on the table
to keep you away

forward

i'm afraid i might shrink in a corner
under the weight of 'what if,'
unravelling all that once felt warm
as doubts from the dark tear me apart

i miss putting in the effort and lose my fight
while dreams dissolve on the first rain's night

forward

hoping to be worthy of changing the beauty of silence

forward

nandini tiwari

i am grateful for the comfort in the shelter of my
strength
worshiping thunder with an unclad mind
distracted by the treasure i held as a child

forward

nandini tiwari

souls escape disappointment
trusting in the honest eyes
that never deceive

forward

i long to steal a flower's grace
for confidence sparks the magic of growth
where the finest self unfurls in silence

forward

doubt lingers, a shadow unseen
trust and truth now dance in my dream
i believed you, thought you were true
but forgot it was all just a view

forward

amid rustling pages and the scent of old books
every glance was a chapter, and time softly shook

hearts began to rush, calling love gently
like a whispered dream
making every heartbeat a timeless theme

forward

nandini tiwari

in that touch
the colours of the rainbow became an endless cycle
shielding it from the disappointment
hidden in silent devotion

forward

nandini tiwari

souls truly meet by accident
for my dreams are richer than reality's glance

forward

nandini tiwari

in the space between the words unsaid
we stand on lines we dare not cross, fearing loss

forward

only if promises stayed true and roses bloomed
would we destroy love halfway out the door

forward

as the days stretched into night
the spark i thought was there took flight
in my heart, clear as day
i knew i couldn't, couldn't stay
set me free, i softly plead
let me go, i'll find my way

31

forward

why are we here, i ask aloud
to love in silence, yet feel so proud?
we believe in love, yet close the door
afraid of pain, or something more
is life meant to end alone?
is that the truth we've always known?
or is it more- a quiet tear
crying when we're trapped by fear?
is life two souls who dare to love
or managing ourselves above?
is it passion in the eyes we see
or being fooled by lies, too blind to flee?
is life about holding on so tight
or letting go, and finding light?
i wonder still, what path is right
in this journey through the night

forward

i wished to stay, but now i see
this love will never set us free

forward

how silly of me to adore a charmer
whose words were mere tools
filled with alarm, i now struggle to rise
am i truly failing, or just lost in my own disguise?

forward

i understand now that the universe connects us
not merely through the passage of time
but through the warmth
that lets our skin recognize one another

forward

memories return, like secrets we keep
it's alright to chase what once was lost
sometimes the journey is worth the cost

forward

i cherish with time, she adores with a smile
in the spaces between, we find our own language
a silent understanding that grows with each glance

forward

a series of little moments, fallen for you
i could commit a crime, it's interesting, it's true
in the dance of the heart, where choices entwine
every step with you feels like a reason to shine

forward

nandini tiwari

there's no way to say you've been kind
the truth of love is you
and everything that belongs to you is safe

forward

may the sky teach me
what's meant to be, unfolds
like clouds drifting free

forward

it's been years, but i still crave silence
silently hoping time made a mistake
pushing it far away for no one to stay
mistakes linger, leaving me yearning
for a place where peace can settle
and my heart be unburdened

forward

when i read about her leaving
the world split into reasons

still beating

forward

nandini tiwari

sometimes in the light
the right person crosses paths
to show that time, indeed, heals all

forward

between what is and what might be
mid-conversation, our eyes glance quietly
yet, a small sunset stroll is all we share
is it the conversations that attack
or am i just afraid to let it stay?

forward

we both know love can't rewrite the night

forward

sometimes it's just a moment
all penned down tight

forward

may you look back with a smile
as she writes you into her story
dreaming of magic, holding tight
to moments once near, forever bright

forward

it's okay to take your time
one more chance, one more breath

just conversations that need nothing
but your presence

forward

with them, i'll chase the summer skies
it seems too odd to fantasize
for in their arms, my heart anew
finds every dream it never knew

forward

in love's each chapter
you are the piece that brings meaning
to the quiet spaces
lasting through the years
for tears once unloved

forward

here's a secret, sweet and true
of a timeless dance

in every memory, our story's told
from young to old, a love unfolds

forward

we are wild creatures
forever is too long to adore

so we dance, carefree
knowing it was never meant to be

with a beauty untold, our bond remains strong
yet no chains bind us by night
for this love was never meant for light

forward

what was once alive is now distant and old
just stories untold
in stillness, it sounds like whispers of gold
i wish to melt the snow
to live once more the days that were bright
with all that i used to know

forward

i linger now with words unsaid
maybe too long for what i'll never know
silence hangs between us, thick and still
for i know you'll blame me for a restless mind
i know you will
doubt clouds the air, for i ache to speak
if i were not tired and weak

it'll be me
i'd let the silence break, afraid of the truth
which may be a mistake
so we stay, with hearts full and on display
for others to find their way

forward

55

you stand a mystery
a whisper so bold
yet a heart so old
i love to play
for the thrill of your chase
and the spark in your eyes
to believe that love
is all that we weave

forward

i wish to live in the warmth of your presence
without counting the cost, where time is lost

you hold a trace of my feelings sold
now, only in dreams, our story unfolds

forward

and i won't let it all fall

i've danced with the doubts, embraced every call
to be what's known as fierce and strong
if it's cared for to rise
i'll stay to write my own song

forward

nandini tiwari

i drew it to her light, in happiness
and now the stars shine bright

forward

i am never clean—the price of a soft heart
it's both bitter and sweet

so i carry my heart with love
as a plan in the mess of it all

forward

not only when you were burdened or lost did i hold
you close
i was always there, where you truly belong
together, never alone

forward

allow me to care for you
caught between the roles you play
let me hold the weight you carry
beneath expectations, i swear
the parts of you that don't quite fit
i'll carry too
for what you've given me is enough
i only see you

forward

in this vast world, i'm lost and alone
i've kept myself busy, forgotten the tone
now i'm unknown, beyond chaos that sang me to
sleep
but all is not lost, for love is what we keep

forward

do you remember that fire in our souls
the one that once made us feel whole?
now it flickers, reminding us
that passion carries its embers
while love brings its responsibilities

forward

forward

each thought of your smile, i can't now explain
in dreams i hold it like a whisper through the haze
i wish i could capture the light it brought
to carry with me when everything felt wrong

nandini tiwari

65

it took me time to understand you
your presence is bittersweet, yet a relief

forward

though your absence cuts deep like a knife
it's now a testament to the beauty we shared
it's equal to a weight
but at least it's not love
the laughter
the dreams
woven into our days

forward

i'll create a new world
both different and true
for to lie within it
is a choice i refuse

i've waited long enough
for the heart to speak
but once again, silence remains
like a half-finished story

forward

if you have the ability to hold
then no matter how long i bear the weight
in hope for the morning rays
i will wait
i will stand beneath the starless skies
even when the glaring eyes and whispers in silence
walk along
i will carry the song

only if you…

forward

nandini tiwari

i may never find what makes you happy
but i would stay, for there are ways to try
in the searching, love won't die

forward

i hope you find the moments that change you
for the mistakes you've made
or the bedtime stories replaced
truly discover yourself
a stranger in the mirror of time
live holding each memory

for it's both a blessing and a curse
the time of your life

forward

nandini tiwari

stop choosing to be cherished
different minds shape your thoughts

what does that say?
drown in whispers that clone you
a shadow molded by others

forward

words linger on the edge of lips
like secrets tucked in the folds of a map
waiting to uncover unexplored lands
where untold stories and desires abide

forward

nandini tiwari

in the quiet of dusk, with time and grace
i look forward to the stars and their glow
leaving our memories in them, i take with me

a cherished token
sunsets as souvenirs, softly spoken

forward

in the silence of night where souls collide
thoughts spill out before we can deny
dreams woven in shadows and in these words our
hearts find home

forward

nandini tiwari

in this present moment
where hearts beat in unison
the future feels uncertain
hope dances through the pain
painting with the glance of promises
or the touch of refrain

all of this, to only be
calling the walls to be unmade

forward

if i had known
how to keep promises
i would still find comfort
in my loneliness
because time
my greatest enemy
would continue
to slip away

forward

some days
love doesn't balance evenly
but the spaces we find together, are the treasures
we deserve
on this shared journey, between our two worlds

not so little things

forward

i've become a wanderer of rainbows
my dreams paint your story, with vibrant hues
still waiting to be complete
where the heart hides and whispers of love linger

forward

i vow not to dictate my fate
for love's weight teaches me the beauty in each
breath
the gold is found in living from the heart

forward

i think
the universe whispers

love is a sacred longing
dividing pleasure from lust
into fleeting moments
where no one truly wins
but still
it holds the greatest value

forward

i wish to know
why are we all different
yet similar?

the way we talk
about broken compliments
is it because we all break apart
in silence?

pieces scatter, like shared secrets
as we're holding on the same thread
afraid to lose what we've made

but still we gather and hide
to win the glue of kindness before time

forward

if only it had been you
holding memories
soft and true

when the nights grew still
i would reach for you
letting feelings gently flow
like whispers in the dark

if only it had been you

forward

oh, but don't worry about me

now i whisper softly, "i'm fine"
if love is meant for me alone
i fear i might be wrong

i tell myself this often
yet in quiet moments
i still search for where i belong

forward

life changes
but don't worry
you were the spark
where every story begins
and your essence lingers
in every heartbeat, every memory
a gentle reminder
love remains
even as the seasons shift
for you were true and beautiful
to them in every sense

forward

isn't it funny
how love can be so strange?
it wraps us in doubt and ties us in knots
i wish i could love
without carrying the weight
yet still
i long for what could have been
because the heart finds beauty
in the things it cannot change

forward

in the quiet of night
i wonder and wait
my fingers trace doubt
through memories
that taste bittersweet
in the mirror
i search for a sign
was it just time?
the questions linger
in the shadows
between what was right
and what was wrong
you feel like a distant song

forward

i wait in stillness
watching countless miracles drift by
each one a gift
and i long for one
selfish, maybe
but even the sky must darken
for a star to shine bright

there's peace in not knowing, i agree
yet even if moments were meant to pass
some things linger

as night fades to day
my darling, it's okay to stay

forward

you were the star
i never knew i'd wish upon
but now, you're the one
i long to hold forever
from that day, every wish i make
is a promise to never fade
i don't know how the rays
echo your name
you've become the warmth in my cold
a story definitely to be told

forward

hold my hand
we have stories to tell
in this endless night
where dreams come alive
let the world rush by
while we stand still
wrapped in our tales
beneath the stars
in the words we say
together we dream
without a single care

forward

in the paths we once walked
each corner holds a memory
silence wraps around me, like whispers

i hold onto a love
that wasn't a lesson
just a moment
frozen in time

the unspoken
now echoes softly
in my heart

forward

your presence is comfort
not just in the warmth of love
but in the quiet moments

when we simply are
always here
always patient
a steady heartbeat
like gentle noise

forward

because you deserve that

forward

nandini began writing poetry at ***sixteen***, captivated by the
feeling of creating new worlds through her words
she holds the record for being the youngest to write the most
poetry books as recognized by both
the India Book of Records and the International Book of Records
through her art, nandini hopes to be remembered for her
independence
this book marks her ***sixth collection of poetry***
in addition to her writing, she is active in the community,
running a non-profit organization called "For Us"

-about the author

here's to you
always choosing you
even if i don't

9 7 9 8 8 9 5 5 6 8 5 7 6